Glitter When Yo

Fiona Waters is well known in the world of children's books. She ran Heffers Children's Bookshop for several years and was Editorial Director of School Book Fairs for ten years up to 1996. She now works freelance as a writer and anthologist and provides the book selection for Troubadour.

Also available from Macmillan

Love
Poems chosen by Fiona Waters

Golden Apples
Poems chosen by Fiona Waters

Read Me 1
A Poem for Every Day of the Year
Poems chosen by Gaby Morgan

Read Me 2
Poems chosen by Gaby Morgan

Glitter When You Jump

Poems Celebrating
Girls and Women

Chosen by Fiona Waters

MACMILLAN CHILDREN'S BOOKS

First published 1996 by Macmillan Children's Books
This edition published 2002 by Macmillan Children's Books
a division of Macmillan Publishers Limited
20 New Wharf Road, London N1 9RR
Basingstoke and Oxford
www.panmacmillan.com

Associated companies throughout the world

ISBN 0 330 39991 8

This collection copyright © Fiona Waters 1996

The right of Fiona Waters to be identified as the
compiler of this book has been asserted by her in accordance
with the Copyright, Designs and Patents Act 1988.

All rights reserved. No part of this publication may be
reproduced, stored in or introduced into a retrieval system, or
transmitted, in any form, or by any means (electronic, mechanical,
photocopying, recording or otherwise) without the prior written
permission of the publisher. Any person who does any unauthorized
act in relation to this publication may be liable to criminal prosecution
and civil claims for damages.

1 3 5 7 9 8 6 4 2

A CIP catalogue record for this book is available from the British Library.

Printed by Mackays of Chatham plc, Chatham, Kent.

This book is sold subject to the condition that it shall not,
by way of trade or otherwise, be lent, re-sold, hired out,
or otherwise circulated without the publisher's prior consent
in any form of binding or cover other than that in
which it is published and without a similar condition including
this condition being imposed on the subsequent purchaser.

Contents

Pink-cheeked Little Monsters

My Nearly Best Friend

Do I Look Unhappy But Beautiful?

Women Can Be Burglars Too

Terraced, Tescoed Prisoners

The Sorrows of Your Changing Face

I Thought I Could Deal with Funerals

Pink-cheeked
Little Monsters

For an Unborn Baby

If she's a girl,
I hope she'll stretch her wings
and grow up free, wide ranging
like a seagull, dealing with the winds
competently, swifting on currents of air,
able to live on anything she can find
in the murky sea, or even on rubbish heaps,
adapting with ease when storms drive her inland.
May she choose wisely if in the end
she settles on one name, one piece of ground.

May she banish those who'd seek to protect her
from heartbreak, or joy.
– And may he achieve no less
if he's a boy.

Janet Shepperson

The Meeting Place

(after Rubens: The Adoration of the Magi *1634)*

It was the arrival of the kings
that caught us unawares;
we'd looked in on the woman in the barn,
curiosity you could call it,
something to do on a cold winter's night;
we'd wished her well –
that was the best we could do, she was in pain,
and the next thing we knew
she was lying on the straw
– the little there was of it –
and there was this baby in her arms.

It was, as I say, the kings
that caught us unawares . . .
Women have babies every other day,
not that we are there –
let's call it a common occurrence though,
giving birth. But kings
appearing in a stable with a
'Is this the place?' and kneeling,
each with his gift held out towards the child!

They didn't even notice us.
Their robes trailed on the floor,
rich, lined robes that money couldn't buy.
What must this child be
to bring kings from distant lands
with costly incense and gold?
What could a tiny baby make of that?

And what were we to make of
was it angels falling through the air,
entwined and falling as if from the rafters
to where the gaze of the kings met the child's
– assuming the child could see?

What would the mother do with the gifts?
What would become of the child?
And we'll never admit there are angels

or that somewhere between
one man's eyes and another's
is a holy place, a space where a king could be
at one with a naked child,
at one with an astonished soldier.

Christopher Pilling

Clinic Day

Her thin puny little body,
contorted in rage and indignation.
As I placed her in the cold white scoop,
Of the plastic scales.
The self-satisfied clinic mothers,
dangled their fat, round-faced,
pink-cheeked little monsters.
And gleefully compared notes.
'My little Wayne is taking eight ounces of his feed.'
'He has all his milk teeth has our Arnold.'
'John can count backwards in Urdu.'

I retrieved my scarlet-faced, toothless, wailing
   banshee.
'How many ounces does she take of her feed,'
enquired Mrs Neat as a new pin.
'I'm not sure, she's breast-fed,' I apologized.
A withering look of distaste followed by,
'Oh, I always like to see EXACTLY,
how much Nigel is taking.'
Exit inferior mother,
with squalling inferior infant.
Social Worker 'Isn't she walking yet at 15 months?'
'Er no, I'm afraid not.'
'Perhaps if you had all carpet, in the hall and dining
   room,
she wouldn't be afraid of falling.'
Em tucked one leg under her,
in a sitting position,

and scooted crab-like across the room,
in a defiant gesture, that's my girl!

Jo Barnes

Brother

I had a little brother
And I brought him to my mother
And I said I want another
Little brother for a change.
But she said don't be a bother
So I took him to my father
And I said this little bother
Of a brother's very strange.

But he said one little brother
Is exactly like another
And every little brother
Misbehaves a bit he said.
So I took the little bother
From my mother and my father
And I put the little bother
Of a brother back to bed.

Mary Ann Hoberman

Small Incident in Library

The little girl is lost among the books.
Two years old maybe, in bobble cap,
White lacy tights, red coat. She stands and looks.
'Can't see you, Mummy.' Mummy, next row up,
Intent on reading, answers absently:
'I'm here, love.' Child calls out again: 'Can't see.'

A large man, his intentions of the best,
Stoops: 'Where's Mummy, then?' Child backs away.
Now the tall shelves threaten like a forest.
She toddles fast between them, starts to cry,
Takes the next aisle down and as her mother
Rounds one end disappears behind the other.

I catch the woman's tired-eyed prettiness.
We smile, shake heads. The child comes back in
  sight,
Hurtles to her laughing, hugs her knees:
'Found you!', in such ringing pure delight
It fills the room, there's no one left who's reading.
The mother looks down, blinking. 'Great soft thing.'

David Sutton

A Birthday Poem For Rachel

For every year of life we light
a candle on your cake
to mark the simple sort of progress
anyone can make,
and then, to test your nerve or give
a proper view of death,
you're asked to blow each light, each year,
out with your own breath.

James Simmons

There Was a Little Girl

There was a little girl
Who had a little curl
Right in the middle of her forehead.
When she was good
She was very, very good,
But when she was bad she was horrid.

Henry Wadsworth Longfellow

My Nearly Best Friend

Best Friends

It's Susan I talk to not Tracey,
Before that I sat next to Jane;
I used to be best friends with Lynda
But these days I think she's a pain.

Natasha's all right in small doses,
I meet Mandy sometimes in town;
I'm jealous of Annabel's pony
And I don't like Nicola's frown.

I used to go skating with Catherine,
Before that I went there with Ruth;
And Kate's so much better at trampoline:
She's a show-off, to tell you the truth.

I think that I'm going off Susan,
She borrowed my comb yesterday;
I think I might sit next to Tracey,
She's my nearly best friend: she's OK.

Adrian Henri

Conversation

Why are you always tagging on?
You ought to be dressing dolls
Like other sisters.

Dolls! You know I don't like them.
Cold, stiff things lying so still.
Let's go to the woods and climb trees.
The crooked elm is the best.
From the top you can see the river
And the old man hills,
Hump-backed and hungry
As ragged beggars.
In the day they seem small and far away
But at night they crowd closer
And stand like frowning giants.
Come on! What are you waiting for?

I have better things to do.

It's wild in the woods today.
Rooks claw the air with their cackling.

The trees creak and sigh.
They say that long ago, slow Sam the woodcutter
Who liked to sleep in the hollow oak,
Was found dead there.
The sighing is his ghost, crying to come back.
Let's go and hear it.

I hate the sound

You mean you're afraid?

Of course not.
Jim and I are going fishing.

Can I come too?

What do you know about fishing?
You're only a girl.

Olive Dove

A Touch of Class

When Miss asks a question,
If you're a girl in the class
There's no point in putting your hand up,
Not worth bothering to stand up.
Might as well bring a big brass band up!

Some boy will just call out
Or boorishly bawl out,
Or spray the atomic fall-out
Of his unthought answer – right or wrong.
A girl may sit with her hand up
All day long
                    But Miss
Will not take the slightest notice.

John Kitching

Mary Had a Crocodile

Mary had a crocodile
That ate a child each day;
But interfering people came
And took her pet away.

Anon

Childhood

I used to think that grown-up people chose
To have stiff backs and wrinkles round their nose,
And veins like small fat snakes on either hand,
On purpose to be grand.
Till through the banisters I watched one day
My great-aunt Etty's friend who was going away,
And how her onyx beads had come unstrung.
I saw her grope to find them as they rolled;
And then I knew that she was helplessly old,
As I was helplessly young.

Frances Cornford

For Rita with Love

You came home from school
on a special bus
full of people
who look like you
and love like you
and you met me
for the first time
and you loved me.
You love everybody
so much that it's not safe
to let you out alone.
Eleven years of love
and trust and time for you to learn
that you can't go on loving like this.
Unless you are stopped
you will embrace every person you see.
Normal people don't do that.
Some Normal people will hurt you
very badly because you do.

Cripples don't look nice
but you embrace them.
You kissed a wino on the bus
and he broke down and cried
and he said 'Nobody has kissed me
for the last 30 years.'
But you did.
You touched my face
with your fingers and said

'I like you.'
The world will never
be ready for you.
Your way is right
and the world will
never be ready.

We could learn everything
that we need to know
by watching you
going to your special school
in your special bus
full of people
who look like you
and love like you
and it's not safe
to let you out alone.
If you're not normal
there is very little hope
for the rest of us.

Pat Ingoldsby

Silverly

Silverly,
      Silverly
Over the
      Trees
The moon drifts
      By on a
Runaway
      Breeze.

Dozily,
      Dozily,
Deep in her
      Bed,
A little girl
      Dreams with the
Moon in her
      Head.

Dennis Lee

Paint

A dumpy plain-faced child stands gazing there,
One hand laid lightly on a purple chair.
Her stuffed and stone-grey gown is laced with black;
A chain, with pendant star, hangs round her neck.
Red bows deck wrist and breast and flaxen hair;
Shoulder to waist's a band of lettered gold.
Round eyes, a cupid mouth – say, seven years old;
The ghost of her father in her placid stare.
Darkness beyond; bold lettering overhead:
L'INFANTA, MARGUERITE, there I read;
And wondered – tongue-tied mite, and shy, no
   doubt –
What grave Velásquez talked to her about.

Walter de la Mare

Little Miss Muffet

Little Miss Muffet
sat on her tuffet
eating her butties with Bert.

A spider crawled on her hand:
she picked it up and
shoved it straight down the back of his shirt.

Dave Calder

Do I Look Unhappy But Beautiful?

Marigolds

I bought a bottle of Nettle Shampoo
      this morning.
When I got home I wondered whether
      I shouldn't shampoo
      the marigolds
      as well.

Adrian Henri

A Short Note on Schoolgirls

Schoolgirls are heroes –
they have so many things to pass:
exams, notes in class, hockey balls –
and great big men on building sites
who go WOOAR.

Alison Campbell

Mothers Who Don't Understand

'Why can't you tidy your room?' they cry,
Millions of mothers who fret round the land,
'It's a horrible mess, I've never seen worse,'
– Mothers who don't understand.

They don't understand how cosy it is
To have piles of books on the floor,
And knickers and socks making friends with the vest
Under the bed, where they like it best,
And notices pinned to the door.

They don't understand why Kylie and Craig
Are smiling all over the walls,
And toffees and Chewys and dozen of Smarties
Are scattered about reminding of parties,
And jeans are rolled into balls.

They don't understand why a good bed should be
All scrumpled and friendly and gritty,
Why the bears and the paints and the toys are much
    less
Easy to find if there isn't a mess –
To tidy would be a great pity.

They don't understand the point of a desk
Is to balance the muddle quite high:
To leave the drawers open, grow mould
    on the drink
Is very much easier, some people think,
Than explaining to mothers just why.

'PLEASE can you tidy your room?' they wail,
Millions of mothers who fret round the land:
'What will you do when there's no one to nag you?'
– Mothers who don't understand.

Augusta Skye

Today

Today I will not live up to my potential.
Today I will not relate well to my peer group.
Today I will not contribute in class.
   I will not volunteer one thing.
Today I will not strive to do better.
Today I will not achieve or adjust or grow enriched or
   get involved.
I will not put up my hand even if the teacher is
   wrong and I can prove it.

Today I might eat the eraser off my pencil.
I'll look at clouds.
I'll be late.
I don't think I'll wash.

I need a rest.

Jean Little

For Heidi with Blue Hair

When you dyed your hair blue
(or at least, ultramarine
for the clipped sides, with a crest
of jet-black spikes on top)
you were sent home from school

because, as the headmistress put it,
although dyed hair was not
specifically forbidden, yours
was, apart from anything else,
not done in the school colours.

Tears in the kitchen, telephone calls
to school from your freedom-loving father:
'She's not a punk in her behaviour;
it's just a style.' (You wiped your eyes,
also not in a school colour.)

'She discussed it with me first –
we checked the rules.' 'And anyway, Dad,
it cost twenty-five dollars.
Tell them it won't wash out –
not even if I wanted to try.'

It would have been unfair to mention
your mother's death, but that
shimmered behind the arguments.
The school had nothing else against you;
the teachers twittered and gave in.

Next day your black friend had hers done
in grey, white and flaxen yellow –
the school colours precisely:
an act of solidarity, a witty
tease. The battle was already won.

Fleur Adcock

Sally

She was a dog-rose kind of girl:
elusive, scattery as petals;
scratchy sometimes tripping you like briars.
She teased the boys
turning this way and that, not to be tamed
or taught any more than the wind.
Even in school the word 'ought'
had no meaning for Sally.
On dull days
she'd sit quiet as a mole at her desk
delving in thought.
But when the sun called
she was gone, running the blue day down
till the warm hedgerows prickled the dusk
and moths flickered out.

Her mother scolded; Dad
gave her the hazel-switch,
said her head was stuffed with feathers
and a starling tongue.
But they couldn't take the shine out of her.
Even when it rained
you felt the sun saved under her skin.
She'd a way of escape
laughing at you from the bright end of a tunnel,
leaving you in the dark.

Phoebe Hesketh

Teenage Party

Hello! Come in, they're all in there.
Laura, who's your lad?
Doesn't matter, we'll smuggle him in,
Just don't tell my dad.
Turn it down! Oh, hi there, Gemma.
Great, you brought some booze,
I'll take your coat, and give me that.
It's this way to the loos.
Hey Lizzie, go and talk to Tom,
He does, it's not a lie.
Look over there, he's by himself,
Go for it! Don't be shy.
Troy, don't chuck the crisps around,
They're everywhere, you louse.
You're not going anywhere
'Til you've tidied up this house.
Oh God, Mum, go upstairs,
Everything's under control.
Trust me, yeh, it's going well,
Sort of, on the whole.
What was that! Something smashed.
Nick's bleeding did you say?
Oh no, the priceless china bowl.
Nick, are you OK?
Careful with that beer, Huw,
The sheepskin rug! Stop!
Tobin, get the doorbell,
Huw, get the frigging mop.
When is it going to end?

Another hour at least.
Let's put some quiet music on,
And try to get some peace.
Who's that lying on the floor?
What? Your name is Chris?
Chris who? I wonder,
You're not on my list.
Yes Mum, I've swept the pieces up,
You look like you've been sick.
Parents here? Whose? Oh,
Has anyone seen Suzie and Nik?
Dad, there's a chauffeur at the door,
Shall I send him on his way?
He won't go without a fiver,
Give me some money and I'll pay.
Who's been sick? Where?
I just don't care any more.
Tell the lout to clear it up
And get up from the floor.
Only five more people left
And they're all in the same car.
Oh, except for the two train-missers
Chris someone-or-other and Karl.
Dial-a-Cab should be here soon,
One-thirty I think they said.
Then everyone will've gone home
And I can go to bed.

Rosie Bray (14)

My Sister Betty

My sister Betty said,
'I'm going to be a famous actress.'
Last year she was going to be a missionary.
'Famous actresses always look unhappy but beautiful.'
She said, pulling her mouth sideways
And making her eyes turn upwards
So they were mostly white.
'Do I look unhappy but beautiful?'
'I want to go to bed and read,' I said.
'Famous actresses suffer and have hysterics,'
    she said.
'I've been practising my hysterics.'
She began going very red and screaming
So that it hurt my ears.
She hit herself on the head with her fists
And rolled off my bed on to the lino.
I stood by the wardrobe where it was safer.
She got up saying, 'Thank you, thank you,'
And bowed to the four corners of my bedroom.
'Would you like an encore of hysterics?' she asked.
'No,' I said from inside the wardrobe.
There was fluff all over her vest.
'If you don't clap enthusiastically,' she said,
'I'll put your light out when you're reading.'
While I clapped a bit
She bowed and shouted, 'More, more!'
Auntie Gwladys shouted upstairs,
'Go to bed and stop teasing our Betty.'

'The best thing about being a famous actress,'
    Betty said,
'Is that you get to die a lot.'
She fell to the floor with a crash
And lay there for an hour and a half
With her eyes staring at the ceiling.
She only went away when I said,
'You really look like a famous actress
Who's unhappy but beautiful.'
When I got into bed and started reading,
She came and switched off my light.
It's not much fun
Having a famous actress for a sister.

Gareth Owen

Would You Believe It?

– Jacky's going out with Peter –
– Which one? Not the one with spots –
– No of course not, Peter DAVIS –
– Don't believe you
                    how d'you know? –
– Tracy told me but you mustn't say
I said so –
                    'course not
how did she find out? –
– Well,
Philippa, that's Tracy's mate the one in 3G
her mate Mandy's sister Carol's
best friend Susan and her boyfriend
(his name's Peter)
saw them
                    Coming Out The Pictures

(But you mustn't tell A SOUL)
'cos Jacky's also going out
with someone else as well . . .

Mick Gowar

Women Can Be
Burglars Too

Goodbye

He said
goodbye.
I shuffled
my feet
and kept a close
watch on my
shoes.
He was talking
I was listening
but he probably
thought I was
not
because I never
even lifted my
head.
I didn't want him
to see
the mess mascara
makes when it
runs.

Carol-Anne Marsh

The Passionate Shepherd
to His Love

Come live with me and be my love,
And we will all the pleasures prove,
That hills and valleys, dales and fields,
And all the craggy mountains yield.

There we will sit upon the rocks,
And see the shepherds feed their flocks,
By shallow rivers to whose falls
Melodious birds sing madrigals.

And I will make thee beds of roses
With a thousand fragrant posies,
A cap of flowers, and a kirtle
Embroidered all with leaves of myrtle;

A gown made of the finest wool
Which from our pretty lambs we pull;
Fair linèd slippers for the cold,
With buckles of the purest gold;

A belt of straw and ivy buds,
With coral clasps and amber studs:
And if these pleasures may thee move,
Come live with me and be my love.

The shepherds' swains shall dance and sing
For thy delight each May morning:
If these delights thy mind may move,
Then live with me and be my love.

Christopher Marlowe

The Door

When she suddenly came in
It seemed the door could never close again,
Nor even did she close it – she, she –
The room lay open to a visiting sea
Which no door could restrain.

Yet when at last she smiled, tilting her head
To take her leave of me,
Where she had smiled, instead
There was a dark door closing endlessly,
The waves receded.

Robert Graves

Typewriting Class

Dear Miss Hinson
I am spitting
in front of my top ratter
With the rest of my commercesnail sturdy students
Triping you this later.
The truce is Miss Hinson
I am not hippy wiht my cross.
Every day on Woundsday
I sit in my dusk
With my type rutter
Trooping without lurking at the lattice
All sorts of weird messengers
To give one exam pill,
'The quick down socks . . .
The quick brine pox . . .
The sick frown box . . .
The sick down jocks
Humps over the hazy bog'
When everyone kows
That a sick down jock
would not be seen dead
Near a hazy bog.
Another one we tripe is:
'Now is the tame
For all guide men
To cram to the head
Of the pratty.'
To may why of sinking
I that is all you get to tripe

In true whelks of sturdy
Then I am thinking of changing
To crookery classes.
I would sooner end up a crook
Than a shirt hand trappist
Any die of the wink.
I have taken the tremble, Miss Hinson
To trip you this later
So that you will be able
To understand my indignation.
I must clothe now
As the Bill is groaning

Yours fitfully . . .

Gareth Owen

Pregnant

It's odd becoming a house
inside a shawl,
cells mass
in building-blocks,
rig plumbing,
central heating, wiring, food.

It's a code
reaching back through sky.
We are made from dust
and bone,
constructed from stars
and supernovas,
dreams and chromosomes,
galaxies and ashes.

Skin-silks folded
and wrapped
over skeins of veins,
knotted threads
and membranes thinned into webs,
this baby floats
in a tiny time-machine,

stores
the history of the world.

Isobel Thrilling

Burglars

'I heard something downstairs,' she said.
'What was it?' I said.
'I don't know,' she said.
'Maybe it's a noise,' I said.
'Go down and see,' she said.
'You mean, go down and see?' I said.
'Yes,' she said.
'Right now?' I said.
'Yes,' she said.
'It was probably a twig scraping the windows,' I said.
'There are no trees outside our house,' she said.
'I think it has stopped,' I said.
'In that case, go down and see,' she said.
'If it is a burglar,' I said,
'I may disturb him,' I said.
'What do you mean *him*?' she said.
'Women can be burglars too,' she said.

Steve Turner

Green

Sitting in the launderette
Delight and Carol, side by side,
Watching their washing whirl around,
Wishing it was done and dried.

Delight begins to paint her nails
While Carol sits and stares.
First vivid green, then silver specks,
To match the shoes she wears.

Then Carol says, 'That Stan of yours,
He's quite a guy, you know.
We met him down the Rink last week –
That day you didn't go.

He really fancies Eth, he does,
Don't say you hadn't heard.'
Delight begins to paint her toes,
She doesn't say a word.

'I think he asked her for a date –
Of course, I couldn't swear –
He never took his eyes off her,
That day you weren't there.'

Delight gets slowly to her feet,
Walks up to Carol's machine,
Tips the paint in the top of it,
And watches her washing turn green.

Jennifer and Graeme Curry

The Ruined Maid

'O 'Melia, my dear, this does everything crown!
Who could have supposed I should meet you in
   Town?
And whence such fair garments, such prosperi-ty?' –
'O didn't you know I'd been ruined?' said she.

– 'You left us in tatters, without shoes or socks,
Tired of digging potatoes, and spudding up docks;
And now you've gay bracelets and bright feathers
   three!' –
'Yes: that's how we dress when we're ruined,' said
   she.

– 'At home in the barton you said "thee" and
   "thou",
And "thik oon", and "theas oon", and "t'other";
   but now
Your talking quite fits 'ee for high compa-ny!' –
'Some polish is gained with one's ruin,' said she.

– 'Your hands were like paws then, your face blue
   and bleak
But now I'm bewitched by your delicate cheek,
And your little gloves fit on as any la-dy!' –
'We never do work when we're ruined,' said she.

– 'You used to call home-life a hag-ridden dream,
And you'd sigh, and you'd sock; but at present
   you seem
To know not of megrims or melancho-ly!' –
'True. One's pretty lively when ruined,' said she.

– 'I wish I had feathers, a fine sweeping gown,
And a delicate face, and could strut about Town!' –
'My dear – a raw country girl, such as you be,
Cannot quite expect that. You ain't ruined,' said she.

Thomas Hardy

How Do I Love Thee?

How do I love thee? Let me count the ways
I love thee to the depth and breadth and height
My soul can reach, when feeling out of sight
For the ends of Being and ideal Grace.
I love thee to the level of everyday's
Most quiet need, by sun and candle-light.
I love thee freely, as men strive for Right;
I love thee purely, as they turn from Praise.
I love thee with the passion put to use
In my old griefs, and with my childhood's faith.
I love thee with a love I seemed to lose
With my lost saints, – I love thee with the breath,
Smiles, tears, of all my life! – and, if God choose,
I shall but love thee better after death.

Elizabeth Barrett Browning

Solitary Observation Brought Back from a Sojourn in Hell

At midnight tears
Run into your ears.

Louise Bogan

Happily Ever After,

From the Story of the Same Name

He raised his sword
and firmly struck
at the gnarled and ancient wood.
It was harder than he'd thought;
it took several days to clear
the vast entanglement;
but at last he'd made a path
and broken down the door
and she was lovely.
They made the palace
into a sort of museum,
and had gardens properly landscaped.
He soon learnt to understand her
and to love her gentle dependency.
They went visiting relatives
who all spoke so differently anyway
and the language didn't seem to matter.

Later, affairs of state
took up much of his time.
Her attempts at sewing
were almost disastrous
and she couldn't learn the language.
One day, when he was away,
she went back to the old palace,
climbed up to the attic
and fell asleep again.

When they finally heard from him
he sent some money, and wrote
that he'd taken up with seven small miners
and would be gone for some time.

The staff were so relieved
that they didn't even bother to answer the letter.

Janet Dube

Terraced, Tescoed
Prisoners

I am a Mother Cat

My child sleeps beside me –
such happiness.
My child sighs the joys of sleep,
as warm as a small animal,
as happy as a small animal.

She embraces me in her sleep
I am a mother cat,
and she is a little kitten.
I am a mother dog
and she is a little puppy.

In the warm burrow of our bed
our night happiness purrs and sighs.

Anna Swir

The Small Brown Nun

The small brown nun in the corner seat
Smiles out of her wimple and out of her window
Through thick round glasses and through the glass,
And her wimple is white and her habit neat
And whatever she thinks she does not show
As the train jerks on and the low fields pass.

The beer is warm and the train is late
And smoke floats out of the carriage window.
Crosswords are puzzled and papers read,
But the nun, as smooth as a just-washed plate,
Does nothing at all but smile as we go,
As if she listened to something said

Not here, or beyond, or out in the night,
A close friend with a gentle joke
Telling her something through the window
Inside her head, all neat and right
And snug as the white bound round the yolk
Of a small brown egg in a nest in the snow.

Anthony Thwaite

The Heroines

We are the terraced women
piled row upon row on the sagging, slipping hillside
   of our lives.
We tug reluctant children up slanting streets
the pushchair wheels wedging in the ruts.
Breathless and bad-tempered we shift the Tesco
   carrier-bags
from hand to hand
and stop to watch the town.

The hilltops creep away like children playing games.

Our other children shriek against the schoolyard
   rails –
   'There's Mandy's mum, John's mum, Dave's mum,
   Kate's mum, Ceri's mother, Tracey's mummy.'
We wave with hands scarred by groceries and too
   much washing-up
catching echoes as we pass of old wild games.

After lunch, more bread and butter, tea,
we dress in blue and white and pink and white
   checked overalls
and do the house and scrub the porch and sweep the
   street
and clean all the little terraces
up and down and up and down and up and down
   the hill.

Later, before the end-of-school bell rings,
all the babies are asleep
Mandy's mum joins Ceri's mum across the street
  running to avoid the rain
and Dave's mum and John's mum – the others too –
  stop by for tea
and briefly we are wild women
girls with secrets, travellers, engineers, courtesans,
  and stars of fiction, films
plotting our escape like jail-birds
terraced, Tescoed prisoners rising from the
  household dust like heroines.

Penny Windsor

Natural High

my mother is a
red
woman

she
gets high
on clean children

grows
common sense

injects
tales
with heroines

fumes
over dirty habits

hits the sky
on bad lines

crackling meteors

my mother
gets red
with the sun

Jean Binta Breeze

My Christmas: Mum's Christmas

decorations climbing up to the loft
on a wobbly ladder,
probably falling.

a Christmas tree pine needles and tinsel all
over the carpet.

lots of food preparations and loads of
dishes to be washed.

crackers crumpled paper everywhere.

presents money down the drain.

sweets indigestion and tooth-ache.

parties late nights, and driving back
through the dark.

snow to play in getting soaked and frozen
whenever outside.

Sarah Forsyth

Love and Friendship

Love is like the wild rose-briar,
Friendship like the holly-tree
The holly is dark when the rose-briar blooms
But which will bloom most constantly?

The wild rose-briar is sweet in spring,
Its summer blossoms scent the air,
Yet wait till winter comes again
And who will call the wild-briar fair?

Then scorn the silly rose-wreath now
And deck thee with the holly's sheen,
That when December blights thy brow
He still may leave thy garland green.

Emily Brontë

Travel

All day she sits behind a bright brass rail
Planning proud journeyings in terms that bring
　　Far places near; high-coloured words that sing,
'The Taj Mahal at Agra', 'Kashmir's Vale'.
Spanning wide spaces with her clear detail,
　　'Sevilla or Fiesole in spring,
　　Through the fiords in June'. Her words
　　take wing.
She is the minstrel of the great out-trail.

At half-past five she puts her maps away,
　　Pins on a grey, meek hat, and braves the sleet.
A timid eye on traffic. Dully grew
　　The house that harbours her in a grey street,
　　The close, sequestered, colourless retreat
Where she was born, where she will always stay.

Ruth Comfort Mitchell

The Fat Black Woman
Goes Shopping

Shopping in London winter
is a real drag for the fat black woman
going from store to store
in search of accommodating clothes
and de weather so cold

Look at the frozen thin mannequins
fixing her with a grin
and de pretty face salesgals
exchanging slimming glances
thinking she don't notice

Lord is aggravating

Nothing soft and bright and billowing
to flow like breezy sunlight
when she walking

The fat black woman curses in Swahili/Yoruba
and nation language under her breathing
all this journeying and journeying

The fat black woman could only conclude
that when it comes to fashion
the choice is lean

Nothing much beyond size 14

Grace Nichols

Phenomenal Woman

Pretty women wonder where my secret lies.
I'm not cute or built to suit a fashion-model's size
But when I start to tell them,
They think I'm telling lies.
I say,
It's in the reach of my arms,
The span of my hips,
The stride of my step,
The curl of my lips.
I'm a woman
Phenomenally.
Phenomenal woman,
That's me.

I walk into a room
Just as cool as you please,
And to a man,
The fellows stand or
Fall down on their knees.
Then they swarm around me,
A hive of honey bees.
I say,
It's the fire in my eyes,
And the flash of my teeth,
The swing in my waist,
And the joy in my feet.
I'm a woman
Phenomenally.
Phenomenal woman,
That's me.

Men themselves have wondered
What they see in me.
They try so much
But they can't touch
My inner mystery.
When I try to show them
They say they still can't see.
I say,
It's in the arch of my back,
The sun of my smile,
The ride of my breasts,
The grace of my style.
I'm a woman
Phenomenally.
Phenomenal woman,
That's me.

Now you understand
Just why my head's not bowed.
I don't shout or jump about
Or have to talk real loud.
When you see me passing
It ought to make you proud.
I say,
It's in the click of my heels,
The bend of my hair,
The palm of my hand,
The need for my care.
'Cause I'm a woman
Phenomenally.
Phenomenal woman,
That's me.

Maya Angelou

Don't Blame the Bird!

My Aunt Ethelberta's parrot
Is a genius of a bird:
It comes out with strings of language
She insists it's never heard –
Drunkards' oaths, and sailors' curses,
Swearwords that a harassed nurse is
Bound to utter if she drops
A bedpan or a pail of slops . . .
Mum makes me block my ears up fast
When Polly starts to 'damn' and 'blast'.
She begs me never once to speak
The words that issue from that beak.
Aunt Ethelberta looks demure –
'He's not learnt that from me, I'm sure.
However blue may be my mood,
I never let my talk get crude.'
Then Father turns to wink an eye,
Breathing, 'In that case, tell me why
Polly always makes the choice
To swear in Ethelberta's voice!'

Gina Wilson

Our Pier: Orkney

Mrs Jemima Rendall lives in
      the house with the green door.
She keeps twelve hens in her yard
And a fierce red cockerel that
      would leap at you like a flame.

Bella Swann lives in the house with
      the broken window.
She takes in grubby washing
And carries out snow-white layers
      in her basket to the
      lawyers' wives and the
      shopkeepers' wives and the
      minister's wife.

Mrs Roberta Wylie sings all day in
      the house above the sea.
She has six cats
Who all go insane when Tom Wylie
      comes back from the west
      with his boat *Daystar* full
      of fish.

My mother lives in the house next
  the street.
She brightens my face with water
  every morning.
'Now,' she says, 'do what the teacher tells you,
  and you learned your seven times table last
  night – and no fighting with other
  boys, especially Jackie Spence that bully' –
  then she kisses me and gives me a penny.

Miss Audrey Thomas lives in the
  house with lace curtains
And she speaks very proper.
She worked in a lawyer's office in
  Edinburgh for years, now she gives
  piano lessons to the stupid sons
  and daughters of sea captains.

Old Annie Grimsness, she lives in a
  stone hut
But her cabbages and tatties
Are bigger than everyone else's,
  also she can tell what the
  weather will be the day after
  tomorrow, judging by the phase of
  the moon and the piece of dry
  seaweed she keeps on her wall,
  and she's better than any wireless
  weatherman.

George Mackay Brown

The Sorrows of
Your Changing Face

I Have Lived and I Have Loved

I have lived and I have loved;
I have waked and I have slept;
I have sung and I have danced;
I have smiled and I have wept;
I have won and wasted
      treasure;
I have had my fill of pleasure;
And all these things were
      weariness,
And some of them were dreariness.
And all these things – but
      two things
Were emptiness and pain:
And Love – it was the best of them;
And Sleep – worth all the rest
      of them.

Anon

Warning

When I am an old woman I shall wear purple
With a red hat which doesn't go, and doesn't suit
  me,
And I shall spend my pension on brandy and summer
  gloves
And satin sandals, and say we've no money for
  butter.
I shall sit down on the pavement when I'm tired
And gobble up samples in shops and press alarm
  bells
And run my stick along the public railings
And make up for the sobriety of my youth.
I shall go out in my slippers in the rain
And pick the flowers in other people's gardens
And learn to spit.

You can wear terrible shirts and grow more fat
And eat three pounds of sausages at a go
Or only bread and pickle for a week
And hoard pens and pencils and beermats and
  things in boxes.

But now we must have clothes that keep us dry
And pay the rent and not swear in the street
And set a good example for the children.
We must have friends to dinner and read the papers.

But maybe I ought to practise a little now?
So people who know me are not too shocked and
  surprised
When suddenly I am old, and start to wear purple.

Jenny Joseph

Witch

There was this old lady on the bus . . .
  (Old cat! Sourpuss!)
Gave her my hand to pull her on.
'OK, love . . . let me help you, Gran.'
But she hissed and spat like a real old mog . . .
Eye of newt and toe of frog.
(She wasn't a bit like my old Nan
Who smells of cake and apple jam.)
If she'd lived two hundred years ago
They'd have ducked her for a witch, you know.

But then I thought . . .   If her life's been rough,
                      Why – that's enough
                      To make her tough . . .
                      . . . and spitefulhard.
You never can really tell, you see –
In sixty years that might be me.

Marion Lines

Handbag

My mother's old leather handbag,
crowded with letters she carried
all through the war. The smell
of my mother's handbag: mints
and lipstick and Coty powder.
The look of those letters, softened
and worn at the edges, opened,
read, and refolded so often.
Letters from my father. Odour
of leather and powder, which ever
since then has meant womanliness,
and love, and anguish, and war.

Ruth Fainlight

When You Are Old

When you are old and grey and full of sleep,
And nodding by the fire, take down this book,
And slowly read, and dream of the soft look
Your eyes had once, and of their shadows deep;

How many loved your moments of glad grace,
And loved your beauty with love false or true,
But one man loved the pilgrim soul in you,
And loved the sorrows of your changing face;

And bending down beside the glowing bars,
Murmur, a little sadly, how Love fled
And paced upon the mountains overhead
And hid his face amid a crowd of stars.

W. B. Yeats

On Platform 5

I watch you gripping your hands
that have grown into the familiar contours
of old age, waiting for the train
to begin its terrifying journey
back to yourself, to your small house
where the daily habit of being alone
will have to be learnt all over again.

Whatever you do with your lined face
nothing disguises that look in your eyes.
Between you and your family
words push like passengers until
your daughter kisses you goodbye –
uttering those parting platitudes
that spill about the closing of a door.

For them your visit's over and relief
jerks in the hands half-lifted now to wave.
Soon there will be far distances between
and duty letters counting out your year.
A whistle blows. The station moves away.
A magazine stays clenched upon your lap.
And your white knuckles tighten round each fear.

Edward Storey

Rebellion

She ran away from the old people's home.

She sleeps in railway stations,
she tramps the streets, the fields,
shouting, singing, cursing
obscenely.

At the back of her head, behind the orbs of her eyes,
she carries – in the bone reliquary of her skull –
rebellion.

Anna Swir

Granny Granny
Please Comb My Hair

Granny Granny please comb
my hair
you always take your time
you always take such care

You put me on a cushion
between your knees
you rub a little coconut oil
parting gentle as a breeze

Mummy Mummy
she's always in a hurry-hurry
rush
she pulls my hair
sometimes she tugs

But Granny
you have all the time
in the world
and when you're finished
you always turn my head and say
'Now who's a nice girl'

Grace Nichols

Old Mrs Glory Roberts

Old Mrs Glory Roberts
Lives all alone except for her cats.
Her house was once
The best and the biggest,
But now it's all been turned into flats.

Old Mrs Glory Roberts
Waters her herbs in their earthenware pot.
Her garden was once
A flourishing acre,
But now it's only a cat-prowled plot.

Old Mrs Glory Roberts
Sits and laughs in the morning sun,
Calls to her sleek
Soft-stepping companions,
Greets them by name as they come every one.

> 'Come Sheba and Shaftoe and Selim and Sue,
> Millicent, Moggy and Mo,
> Now Barney and Benny, with one-eared Bee,
> And my own little cross-eyed Beau.
> Come Felix, Fenella and Freddy and Flops,
> And Maurice, the one with no tail,
> Then Jingo and Jackie and gentle old Joe,
> Who's fourteen and getting quite frail.'

Old Mrs Glory Roberts
Sits with her friends in the midday glare,
And the air is loud
With the purring they make,
And the milky content that she shares with them there.

Jennifer and Graeme Curry

Gran's Doss House

My Grandma keeps a boarding house;
She takes in lodgers thirty.
Not one of them is over-clean,
And seven are filthy dirty.

Gran sleeps 'em eight to every bed,
And four or five more under.
The lights go out at half past nine,
Or Gran comes up like thunder.

By six a.m. the beds are left,
As men for work make track;
By twenty past the beds are filled:
The night shift men are back!

She feeds them all on cabbage pie,
Black toast and inch-thick pastry.
She keeps a sharp eye round the shops
For nosh that's cheap and nasty.

Gran hardly ever washes up
Till rain falls, I am certain.
She leaves the mucky pots outside,
Then wipes them on a curtain.

She smokes cigars in bed till ten,
Slurps mushy peas and garlic;
And when this lot's swilled down with gin
She lights up like a Dalek;

Lifts from the bath twin crocodiles;
Arms full, downstairs she labours.
She cackles as they roll outside
To terrorize the neighbours.

I only go to see my Gran
When by my Mum I'm bid.
I wouldn't live in Grandma's house
for fifty thousand quid.

Howard Peach

Grannie

I stayed with her when I was six then went
To live elsewhere when I was eight years old.
For ages I remembered her faint scent
Of lavender, the way she'd never scold
No matter what I'd done, and most of all
The way her smile seemed, somehow, to enfold
My whole world like a warm, protective shawl.

I knew that I was safe when she was near,
She was so tall, so wide, so large, she would
Stand mountainous between me and my fear,
Yet oh, so gentle, and she understood
Every hope and dream I ever had.
She praised me lavishly when I was good,
But never punished me when I was bad.

Years later war broke out and I became
A soldier and was wounded while in France.
Back in hospital, still very lame,
I realized that circumstance
Had brought me close to that small town where she
Was living still. And so I seized the chance
To write and ask if she could visit me.

She came. And I still vividly recall
The shock that I received when she appeared
That dark cold day. Huge Grannie was so small!
A tiny, frail, old lady. It was weird.
She hobbled through the ward to where I lay
And drew quite close and, hesitating, peered.
And then she smiled: and love lit up the day.

Vernon Scannell

Measles in the Ark

The night it was horribly dark,
The measles broke out in the Ark;
Little Japheth, and Shem, and all the young Hams,
Were screaming at once for potatoes and clams.
And 'What shall I do,' said poor Mrs Noah,
'All alone by myself in this terrible shower?
I know what I'll do: I'll step down in the hold,
And wake up a lioness grim and old,
And tie her close to the children's door,
And give her a ginger-cake to roar
At the top of her voice for an hour or more;
And I'll tell the children to cease their din,
Or I'll let that grim old party in,
To stop their squeazles and likewise their measles.'
She practised this with the greatest success:
She was everyone's grandmother, I guess.

Susan Coolidge

I Thought I Could Deal
with Funerals

Brass Rubbings

Rubbing black wax on white paper:
The faces of the stately dead rise
Out of the clearly ordered past.

Above, a stone plaque, casually glimpsed,
Then its cut letters tear my eyes:
'Aged six months and twelve days.'

Those twelve days!

Michael Harrison

She Dwelt Among
the Untrodden Ways

She dwelt among the untrodden ways
    Beside the springs of Dove,
A Maid whom there were none to praise
    And very few to love:

A violet by a mossy stone
    Half hidden from the eye
– Fair as a star, when only one
    Is shining in the sky.

She lived unknown, and few could know
    When Lucy ceased to be;
But she is in her grave, and, oh,
    The difference to me!

William Wordsworth

Names

She was Eliza for a few weeks
When she was a baby –
Eliza Lily. Soon it changed to Lil.

Later she was Miss Steward in the baker's shop
And then 'my love', 'my darling', Mother.

Widowed at thirty, she went back to work
As Mrs Hand. Her daughter grew up,
Married and gave birth.

Now she was Nanna. 'Everybody
Calls me Nanna,' she would say to visitors.
And so they did – friends, tradesmen, the doctor.

In the geriatric ward
They used the patients' Christian names.
'Lil,' we said, or 'Nanna',
But it wasn't in her file
And for those last bewildered weeks
She was Eliza once again.

Wendy Cope

Marie Wilson: Enniskillen

Under the statue
        of the Unknown Soldier
a man prepares
        a bomb. He is
an unknown soldier.

The patron saint of warriors
        is Michael.
Between the unknown soldiers
        is a wall.
It is the gable
        of St Michael's Hall.

This was Remembrance Sunday.
        Poppy Day.
They came to hear
        the bugles in the Square.
They did not count
        the unknown soldiers there.

Today there were no sermons.
Unknown soldiers
said later it had not
        gone off as planned.
Under the bricks
        she held her father's hand.

Today there was no Last Post.
         Her last words
were 'Daddy, I love you.'
He said he would trust
God. But her poppy
         lay in the dust.

The protector of unknown soldiers
         is Michael.
The father is at the grave.
         A bell peals.
The name Michael
         means 'God Heals'.

Conor Carson (14)

Test Match Cricket

My mother didn't play cricket,
never watched it
ignored all talk of ashes, ducks and maidens.
In the middle of August she took less interest
in Test Matches than the cat.

Yet when she knew she was dying
and was probably weighing up
the having of children
losing one
reading our way out of the sums
discovering she was someone
people travelled to listen to

she said
I've had a good innings, haven't I?

Michael Rosen

The Lodging-house Fuchsias

Mrs Masters's fuchsias hung
Higher and broader, and brightly swung,
    Bell-like, more and more
Over the narrow garden-path,
Giving the passer a sprinkle-bath
    In the morning.

She put up with their pushful ways,
And made us tenderly lift their sprays,
    Going to her door:
But when her funeral had to pass
They cut back all the flowery mass
    In the morning.

Thomas Hardy

Second Opinion

We went to Leeds for a second opinion.
After her name was called,
I waited among the apparently well
And those with bandages and dark spectacles.

A heavy mother shuffled with bad feet
And a stick, a pad over one eye,
Leaving her children warned in their seats.
The minutes went by like a winter.

They called me in. What moment worse
Than that young doctor trying to explain?
'It's large and growing.' 'What is?' 'Malignancy.'
'Why there? She's an artist!'

He shrugged and said, 'Nobody knows.'
He warned it might spread. 'Spread?'
My body ached to suffer like her twin
And touch the cure with lips and healing sesames.

No image, no straw to support – nothing
To hear or see. No leaves rustling in sunlight.
Only the mind sliding against events
And the antiseptic whiff of destiny.

Professional anxiety –
His hand on my shoulder
Showing me to the door, a scent of soap,
Medical fingers, and his wedding ring.

Douglas Dunn

Until Gran Died

The minnows I caught
lived for a few days in a jar
then floated side-up on the surface.
We buried them beneath the hedge.
I didn't cry, but felt sad inside.

     I thought
     I could deal with funerals
     that is until Gran died.

The goldfish I kept in a bowl
passed away with old age.
Mum wrapped him in a newspaper
and we buried him next to a rose bush.
I didn't cry, but felt sad inside.

     I thought
     I could deal with funerals
     that is until Gran died.

My cat lay stiff in a shoe box
after being hit by a car.
Dad dug a hole and we buried her
under the apple tree.
I didn't cry, but felt *very* sad inside.

     I thought
     I could deal with funerals
     that is until Gran died.

And when she died
I went to the funeral
with relations dressed in black.
They cried, and so did I.
Salty tears ran down my face. Oh, how I cried.

> Yes, I thought
> I could deal with funerals
> that is until Gran died.

She was buried in a graveyard
and even the sky wept that day.
Rain fell and fell and fell
and thunder sobbed far away across the town.
I cried and I cried.

> I thought
> I could deal with funerals
> that is until Gran
> died.

Wes Magee

Epitaph

In 1905, Catherine Alsopp, a Sheffield washerwoman, composed her own epitaph before hanging herself.

Here lies a poor woman who always was tired;
She lived in a house where help was not hired,
Her last words on earth were: 'Dear friends, I am
   going
Where washing ain't done, nor sweeping, nor
   sewing.
But everything there is exact to my wishes,
For where they don't eat, there's no washing of dishes
I'll be where loud anthems will always be ringing
But having no voice, I'll be clear of the singing.
Don't mourn for me now, don't mourn for me never,
I'm going to do nothing for ever and ever.'

Catherine Alsopp

Index of First Lines

Acknowledgements

The compiler and publishers would like to thank the following for permission to reprint the selections in this book. All possible care has been taken to trace the ownership of every selection included and to make full acknowledgement for its use. If any errors have accidentally occurred, they will be corrected in subsequent editions, provided notification is sent to the publishers.

Oxford University Press for 'For Heidi with Blue Hair' by Fleur Adcock from *The Incident Book*; Random House Inc. for 'Phenomenal Woman' by Maya Angelou from *And Still I Rise*. © Maya Angelou 1978; The National Exhibition of Children's Art for 'Teenage Party' by Rosie Bray from the *Cadbury's Ninth Book of Children's Poetry*, 1991; Virago Press Ltd for 'Clinic Day' by Jo Barnes from *Bread and Roses*; Race Today for 'Natural High' by Jean Binta Breeze from *Ryddim Ravings and other poems*; Farrar, Straus and Girouc, Inc. for 'Solitary Observation Brought Back from a Sojourn in Hell' by Louise Bogan from *The Blue Estuaries*. © Louise Bogan 1968; George Mackay Brown for 'Our Pier: Orkney' by George Mackay Brown from *Casting a Spell*; Dave Calder for 'Little Miss Muffet' by Dave Calder; The Penguin Group for 'A Short Note on Schoolgirls' by Alison Campbell from *I Wouldn't Thank You for a Valentine*, Viking, 1992; Conor Carson for 'Marie Wilson: Enniskillen' by Conor

Carson; Faber & Faber Ltd for 'Names' by Wendy Cope from *Serious Concerns*; Hutchinson and the Estate of Frances Cornford for 'Childhood' by Frances Cornford from *Collected Poems*; Jennifer Curry for 'Old Mrs Glory Roberts' and 'Green' from *Down Our Street* by Jennifer and Graeme Curry, Methuen; Olive Dove for 'Conversation' by Olive Dove; The Women's Press for 'Happily Ever After' by Janet Dube from *Dancing the Tightrope*; Faber & Faber Ltd for 'Second Opinion' by Douglas Dunn from *Elegies* 1985; Sinclair Stevenson for 'Handbag' by Ruth Fainlight from *Selected Poems*, published by Hutchinson, 1987; Exely Publications Ltd Watford for 'My Christmas/Mum's Chrismas' by Sarah Forsyth from A *Child's View of Christmas*; HarperCollins for 'Would You Believe It?' by Mick Gowar from *Swings and Roundabouts*. © 1981 Mick Gowar; A. P. Watt Ltd on behalf of The Trustees of the Robert Graves Copyright Trust for 'The Door' by Robert Graves from *Collected Poems*, 1975; Oxford University Press for 'Brass Rubbings' by Michael Harrison from *Junk Mail*; Rogers, Coleridge and White Ltd for 'Best Friends' and 'Marigolds' by Adrian Henri from *The Phantom Lollipop Lady and Other Poems*, Methuen, 1986; The Bodley Head for 'Sally' by Phoebe Hesketh from *A Song of Sunlight*; Gina Maccoby Literary Agency for 'Brother' by Mary Ann Hoberman from *Hello and Goodbye*, Little, Brown and Co., 1959; The O'Brien Press for 'For Rita with Love' by Pat Igoldsby; John Johnson (Author's Agent Ltd) for 'Warning' by Jenny Joseph from *Rose in the Afternoon*; John Kitching for 'A

Touch of Class' by John Kitching from *Our Side of the Playground*, The Bodley Head; Penguin Books Ltd for 'Silvery' by Dennis Lee from *Jelly Belly*, 1983; Watts Books for 'Witch' by Marion Lines from *Tower Blocks*, Watt Books, a division of the Watts Publishing Group; HarperCollins Publishers for 'Today' by Jean Little from *Hey World, Here I am!*; Cambridge University Press for 'Until Gran Died' by Wes Magee from *Morning Break and Other Poems*; The Literary Trustees of Walter de la Mare and the Society of Authors as their representative for 'Paint' by Walter de la Mare; Bristol Broadsides for 'Goodbye' by Carol-Anne Marsh from *Let's Hurry Up*; Ruth Comfort Mitchell for 'Travel' by Ruth Comfort Mitchell from *Welcome to the Party*, BBC Books; Virago Press Ltd for 'The Fat Black Woman Goes Shopping' by Grace Nichols from *The Fat Black Woman's Poems*; Curtis Brown for 'Granny Granny Please Comb My Hair' by Grace Nichols © 1988; HarperCollins Publishers for 'My Sister Betty' and 'Typewriting Class' by Gareth Owen from *Songs of the City*; Howard Peach for 'Gran's Doss House' by Howard Peach; Christopher Pilling for 'The Meeting Place' by Christopher Pilling from *Poems for Christmas*, Peterloo Poets; Scholastic Children's Books for 'Test Match Cricket' by Michael Rosen from *Mind the Gap*; Hutchinson for 'Grannie' by Vernon Scannell from *Love Shouts and Whispers*; The Blackstaff Press for 'For an Unborn Baby' by Janet Shepperson from *Trio 5*; The Gallery Press for 'A Birthday Poem for Rachel' by James Simmons from *Poems 1956–1986*; Augusta Skye for 'Mothers

Who Don't Understand' by Augusta Skye; Edward Storey for 'On Platform 5' by Edward Storey from *A Man in Winter*; The Women's Press from 'Rebellion' and 'I am a Mother Cat' by Anna Swir from *Fat Like The Sun*, 1986; Peterloo Poets for 'Small Incident in Library' by Davis Sutton from *Flints*; Isobel Thrilling for 'Pregnant' by Isobel Thrilling; Curtis Brown for 'The Small Brown Nun' by Anthony Thwaite from *Collected Poems*; Hodder Headline for 'Burglars' by Steve Turner from *The King of Twist*; Penny Windsor for 'The Heroines' by Penny Windsor from *No Holds Barred*; Jonathan Cape for 'Don't Blame the Bird!' by Gina Wilson from *Jim-Jam Pyjamas*.

LoVe

Poems chosen by Fiona Waters

Fiona Waters is a highly accomplished anthologist and a consultant for Troubadour. She has also been a bookseller and a consultant for television and radio.

'Fiona Waters is an experienced, discerning collector who often turns a collection of poems into a work of art'
  Margaret Meek, *Signal Magazine*

Party

Sitting on the stairs
you tell me that when you were five
a boy called David Bird tried to kiss you,
missed and fell into a bed of nettles.

I want to kiss you now,
but what would I fall off.
and what would I fall into?

Too late I move, indecisively,
and fall into the nettles.

Someone takes you gently by the hand,
smooths your hair,
leads you back to the party.

Adrian Henri

A selected list of titles available from Macmillan Books

The prices shown below are correct at the time of going to press. However, Macmillan Publishers reserve the right to show new retail prices on covers which may differ from those previously advertised.

A Nest Full of Stars Poems by James Berry	0 333 96051 3	£9.99
The Fox on the Roundabout Poems by Gareth Owen	0 330 48468 0	£4.99
The Very Best of Paul Cookson Poems by Paul Cookson	0 330 48014 6	£3.99
The Very Best of David Harmer Poems by David Harmer	0 330 48190 8	£3.99
The Very Best of Wes Magee Poems by Wes Magee	0 330 48192 4	£3.99
Scottish Poems Poems chosen by John Rice	0 333 90073 1	£9.99
Golden Apples Poems chosen by Fiona Waters	0 330 29728 7	£3.99
Love Poems chosen by Fiona Waters	0 333 90348 X	£7.99

All Macmillan titles can be ordered at your local bookshop or are available by post from:

Book Service by Post
PO Box 29, Douglas, Isle of Man IM99 1BQ

Credit cards accepted. For details:
Telephone: 01624 675137
Fax: 01624 670923
E-mail: bookshop@enterprise.net

Free postage and packing in the UK.
Overseas customers: add £1 per book (paperback)
and £3 per book (hardback).